What Would You Do If...?

What Would You Do If...?

A Safety Game for You and Your Child

Jeanne Ebert

Illustrations by Laurel Porter

Houghton Mifflin Company · Boston · 1985

Library of Congress Cataloging in Publication Data

Ebert, Jeanne.
What would you do if...?

Bibliography: p.
Summary: Illustrations of common or unusual emergency
situations are presented with blank lines under each
drawing that are to be filled in by parent and child
after they decide what the answer to this particular
problem should be.
1. Children's accidents—United States—Prevention.
2. Safety education—United States. [1. Accidents.
2. Safety]   I. Porter, Laurel, ill.   II. Title
HV675.E24   1985   613.6′008054   84-19720
ISBN 0-395-37023-X (pbk.)

Printed in the United States of America

P   10 9 8 7 6 5 4 3 2 1

Dedicated to
the Safety of All
Children
and Their Parents'
Peace of Mind

Contents

Introduction

From time immemorial, parents have had the responsibility of teaching their children rules of safe behavior appropriate to the age in which they live. These days, as our children spend more time on their own, as streets become busier, neighborhoods more impersonal, and our society more complex and threatening, teaching our children certain rules of safety is more critical than ever.

It is also more difficult. Many of the dangers we see for our children are "new" dangers—we're not always sure how to handle them ourselves. And the more worried *we* are about our children's safety, the more essential it is not to frighten *them* into becoming fearful creatures unable to deal with new experiences and unfamiliar people.

Yet parents need the peace of mind that comes with knowing that a child will behave in a certain prearranged safe way if a potentially dangerous situation arises, whether it involves an everyday action such as crossing a street or an unusual one such as responding to a stranger who offers candy or gum.

That's where the game "What would you do if . . . ?" comes in. For my own family and many of our friends, playing "What would you do if...?" has been a simple but amazingly effective way of preparing children to act in a specific *predetermined* way in virtually any unsafe situation. Because you don't *tell* your children what to do—how often do the things we tell children fall on deaf ears?—but ask them what *they* would do, the children are involved in the decision from the beginning. As they answer your questions and ask their own, they learn the reasons why it's important to behave in certain ways. As you discuss their answers to "What would you do if...?" you show that you value their ideas and welcome their suggestions. The game concludes when the parent and child together decide what the answer to the question should be. That's the answer it should *always* be—whenever you repeat the question. In this way, the child will remember exactly what to do in any given situation, quickly and safely.

As a grade school teacher and mother of a son and daughter, I started playing "What would you do if...?" with my children when they were very young and I was concerned about their safety when they weren't with me. I wanted to prepare them for both everyday hazards and the unpredictable ones. As a teacher, I wanted to help my children stretch their imaginations and learn to think for themselves, and I found that this question-and-answer approach to safety issues did just that. Asking my children what *they* would do if...not only helped them become aware of certain problems, it also helped them gain a feeling of confidence about dealing with them.

One of the questions I discussed with Peter and Lisa was: "What would you do if you lost me in a store?" The answer we agreed on was: "Stay in the store you are lost in. Go to the door you came in by.

If you can't find that door, go to any door and wait."

One day when the family was visiting an unfamiliar city, we lost Peter, who was then four and a half years old. My husband, John, and I had taken different routes and each of us assumed that the other had Peter along. When we joined up and discovered that neither of us had Peter, we ran back to the last store where we'd all been together. There he was, by the door, totally engrossed in a gum-ball machine. "What took you so long?" he demanded. On the way home, John wanted to know how I knew where to look. Peter answered by saying, "It's one of our What Ifs, Dad!"

In the pages that follow, you'll find a variety of "What would you do if...?" questions, illustrated by drawings. When you and your child have agreed upon the correct answer, fill it in exactly as you want it remembered, and let your child color in the drawing. From time to time, review the question and the answer.

Although this *looks* like a child's book, it's really a book for parents and children together; it shouldn't be given to your child to keep or to go through at one sitting. It's best to do one or two questions at a time. If a safety issue comes up that you want to discuss, look it up in the table of contents in the front of the book. Since every family has its own specific needs, I've included blank pages for filling in your own questions and drawings in each section.

In our family, "What would you do if...?" has become a part of our family history. We play it for a serious reason and because it is fun. We don't play only safety games; we often discuss funny circumstances and family situations. When my husband and I were preparing for the birth of our second child, we both hoped it would be a girl. I asked Peter, who was then two and a half, "What would you do if you had a new baby sister?"

"I'd give her back!" was his reply.

"Why would you do that?"

"Because I want a brother like Brian."

Brian was Peter's pal across the street. No amount of prodding or "What would you do if...?" questions could convince Peter to change his mind.

I was somewhat relieved when Lisa was born and we brought her home: Peter seemed genuinely proud to be her brother, and we put him in charge of parading in family and friends to see her. Lisa was a colicky baby and I often had to rock her or walk around the house with her. One morning after a particularly long bout with cramps and crying, Lisa was finally taking a nap, and I collapsed into a chair in the kitchen. Peter came in, put his hand on my knee, and said, "See? I told you we should have got a brother!" Well, you can't win them all.

Recently, at age fourteen, Peter turned the tables on me. He began with, "What would you do if I was having a hard time with French?" and went on to "...if I didn't do well on a test?" and "...if you had to sign a really low test grade?"

I can't say that I wasn't adequately prepared when he brought home the poor grade to be signed!

Lost—and Found!

Sometimes children really are lost, and sometimes they only think they are. There's a world of difference to you, but to a child it's all the same—a thoroughly frightening event. Worse, a child who gets panicky at the idea of being lost may act irrationally and get into deeper trouble.

But the child who knows in advance exactly how to act in order to be "found" won't panic in a particular situation and will be able to remember the answer that you've all agreed upon.

Throughout this book you'll find blank pages following each section for you to use for your own special situations.

WHAT WOULD YOU DO IF...

YOU LOST MOM OR DAD
AT THE SUPERMARKET
OR STORE?

_____

_____

_____

_____

3

When my family goes to the carnival, we always use the Ferris wheel—preferably the double Ferris wheel, if there is one—as our prearranged meeting place. If you choose a special place in answering this question, be sure that "your" spot actually exists and is easily found. Of course, it's a good idea to review your "What would you do if...?" answer before you let go of each other's hands.

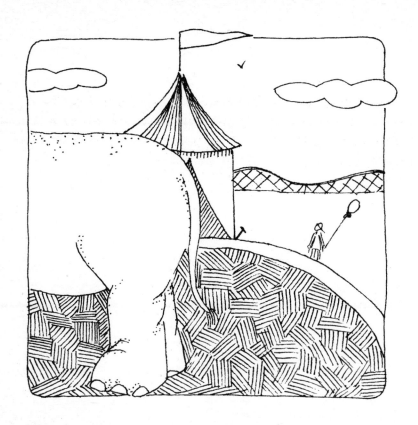

WHAT WOULD YOU DO IF...

YOU LOST MOM OR DAD
AT A CARNIVAL OR FAIR?

_____

_____

_____

_____

Children occasionally stray from their neighborhood. They might be with a group of playmates or just inquisitive about something that needed exploring. Some children are able to get home by thinking backward and retracing their steps. Since you can't count on this, though, you'll want to find a more sure-fire answer to this question.

WHAT WOULD YOU DO IF...

YOU WANDERED TOO FAR
FROM YOUR NEIGHBORHOOD
AND YOU COULDN'T FIND
YOUR WAY HOME?

_____
_____
_____
_____

Getting lost in the woods is easy—and scary. Since there are no familiar landmarks or people around to help, the rules for getting found are different from the ones in the previous examples. Here's some advice for children from one of my teacher colleagues, who is an expert outdoorsman.

- Stay put once you realize you are lost.
- Keep calling for help. But don't panic: someone will look for you as soon as they realize you are missing.
- If you hear any people, move toward them and call out as you go.
- Leave a trail of broken branches or other objects (not food, which can get eaten by animals) in case you want to return to your spot.
- Remember that you will be found.

WHAT WOULD YOU DO IF...

YOU GOT LOST IN THE
WOODS?

_____

_____

_____

_____

WHAT WOULD YOU DO IF...

_____

_____

_____

_____

WHAT WOULD YOU DO IF...

_____

_____

_____

_____

11

WHAT WOULD YOU DO IF...

_____
_____
_____
_____

Cars and Traffic

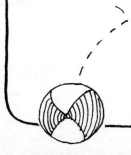

Driver education courses stress that there is a correct way to "look both ways." Both pedestrians and drivers should look first to the *left*, then to the *right*, and then to the *left* again before crossing a street or driving through an intersection. The second look to the left protects you against quickly approaching cars.

WHAT WOULD YOU DO IF...

YOU HAD TO CROSS A
BUSY STREET AND
NO ONE WAS THERE TO
HELP YOU?

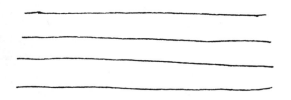

15

Only people who drive cars know how hard it is to see a person who darts into the street from between two parked cars. It's worse, of course, if the pedestrian happens to be small.

WHAT WOULD YOU DO IF...

YOU WANTED TO CROSS
THE STREET AND
THERE WERE CARS
PARKED ALONG THE CURB?

_____

_____

_____

_____

In the excitement of chasing after a ball or a playmate, kids sometimes act as if all rules were suspended. They may remember to look both ways—or think they are looking—but if they don't stop before they look, it could be too late.

WHAT WOULD YOU DO IF...

YOUR BALL ROLLED
INTO THE STREET?

_____

_____

_____

_____

Here's a good way to sneak in a clean-up-after-yourself discussion.

WHAT SHOULD YOU DO WHEN...

YOU ARE FINISHED PLAYING
WITH YOUR OUTSIDE TOYS?

_____

_____

_____

_____

WHAT WOULD YOU DO IF...

_____

_____

_____

_____

22

Temptations

Children are usually told that they should not eat any unwrapped food they find. But what do you want your children to do if they find a piece of *wrapped* food? I don't think you have to scare them with stories about razor blades in apples, but it certainly is important for children to know that it isn't safe to eat food that they come upon accidentally.

WHAT WOULD YOU DO IF...

YOU FOUND SOMETHING GOOD TO EAT ON THE GROUND?

_____

_____

_____

_____

If you want your children to crayon *only* on paper (and who doesn't?), it's up to you to see that paper is available. You may need to be specific when you talk about paper: very young children may not see the difference between the paper in a pad or a coloring book and the paper that we call stationery, wallpaper, napkins, or an adult's book.

WHAT WOULD YOU DO IF...

YOU FOUND CRAYONS BUT
NO PAPER?

_____

_____

_____

27

When it comes to children finding medicines and cleaning solutions, there is absolutely no doubt that *prevention* on the part of adults is the first requirement. But none of us remembers all the time, and children do find these potentially lethal products in other people's houses, so it really isn't safe to skip these questions on the grounds that it can't happen to your child.

WHAT WOULD YOU DO IF...

YOU FOUND MEDICINE
LYING AROUND?

Cleaning solutions are truly dangerous products in the hands of a child. Actually, the *least* dangerous thing a child can do with them is to use them for their proper purpose —to clean. One mother told me how her four-year-old decided to surprise her by washing the floor. It took the mother hours to clean up an inch of water and the contents of a whole box of Spic and Span from the floor.

WHAT WOULD YOU DO IF...

YOU FOUND **SOME** CLEANING SOLUTION AND YOU HAD NOTHING TO DO?

_____

_____

_____

_____

Of course, if we all learned to put away our tools, we wouldn't need this question, would we?

WHAT WOULD YOU DO IF...

YOU FOUND SOME
INTERESTING TOOLS
LYING AROUND?

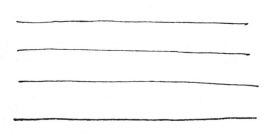

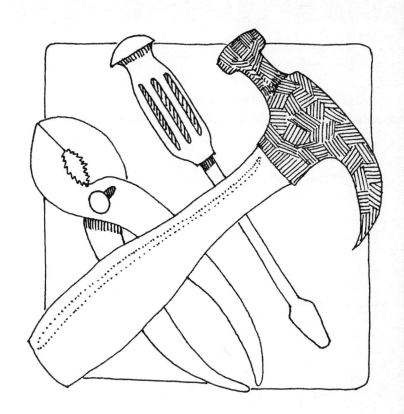

Just one suggestion about your answer here: if you decide that your child should get broken glass out of the way, remember that burying it—especially at the beach—isn't a safe solution. My daughter, Lisa, learned about broken glass the hard way when she stepped on a piece that had been buried in the sand at a beach. Even after emergency treatment at the hospital, it was three years before the last sliver finally worked its way out.

WHAT WOULD YOU DO IF...

YOU FOUND BROKEN GLASS
OUTSIDE?

_____

_____

_____

This picture suggests a different kind of temptation than the previous ones. Here your child probably will be tempted to bop the other kid on the head with the teddy bear. The right answer depends on his or her age and stage of development.

WHAT SHOULD YOU DO IF...

YOUR FRIEND WANTS TO
PLAY WITH THE TOY YOU'RE
PLAYING WITH?

_____

_____

_____

_____

WHAT WOULD YOU DO IF...

_____

_____

_____

_____

WHAT WOULD YOU DO IF...

_____
_____
_____
_____

39

WHAT WOULD YOU DO IF...

_____

_____

_____

_____

Fire Safety

There is probably not one American child who hasn't been told not to play with matches —and probably not a child who hasn't, at some time, experimented with lighting them. Clearly, the lure is stronger than the warning. But the issue is too important to give up on it.

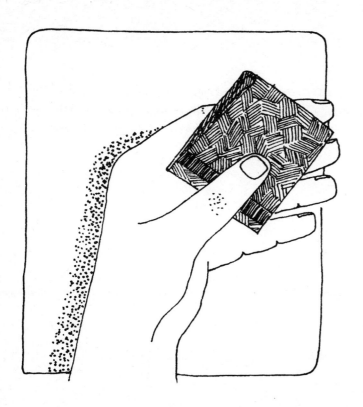

WHAT WOULD YOU DO IF...

YOU FOUND A BOOK OF
MATCHES?

_____

_____

_____

_____

My son, who knows that it's a good idea to stamp out a spark from a fire, was quick to respond one day when a spark landed on our rug. The only trouble was, he stamped it out with a bare foot! It was our fault that we had forgotten how literally children can take us.

WHAT WOULD YOU DO IF...

A SPARK FROM THE
FIREPLACE LANDED ON
THE RUG AND NO ADULT
WAS THERE?

If fire struck your house right now, would you and your family be able to get out safely? Many thousands of lives lost in fires each year could have been saved if there had been active smoke detectors, planned escape routes, and prearranged meeting places outside of the burning building.

Before discussing this important question with your child, stop and plot escape routes for everyone. Anticipate hallways and stairways being blocked. If windows are the only means of escape, are they easy to open? Does your child know how to unlock the windows, including the storm windows? You should use this question to reinforce the plan you have set up for your family.

WHAT WOULD YOU DO IF...

THERE WAS A FIRE IN YOUR HOUSE?

_____

_____

_____

_____

47

With this question and the previous one, I suggest that you actually act out your answers so that they truly will come as second nature should they ever be needed.

WHAT WOULD YOU DO IF...

YOU HAD TO GET OUT OF
YOUR HOUSE DURING A FIRE?

_____

_____

_____

_____

There's only one good answer here. In the event that your child's clothes ever did catch on fire, the child must be taught to stop, drop, and roll. This will smother the fire. If the child panics and runs, it will fan the flames.

Most fires occur when the child is wearing loose clothing, such as pajamas or a nightgown. Check these articles. Make sure they are flame retardant.

WHAT WOULD YOU DO IF...

YOUR CLOTHES CAUGHT
ON FIRE?

_____

_____

_____

_____

WHAT WOULD YOU DO IF...

_____

_____

_____

_____

WHAT WOULD YOU DO IF...

53

WHAT WOULD YOU DO IF...

_____
_____
_____
_____

Appliances

Even a child who knows about fire may not realize the hazards of boiling liquids. I know a parent who would have much preferred to have had to clean up a scorched pot than have had her child undergo twenty-seven operations for burns suffered as a result of trying to turn off the stove.

WHAT WOULD YOU DO IF...

YOU FOUND SOMETHING
BUBBLING OVER ON THE
STOVE AND NOBODY WAS
IN THE KITCHEN?

Fire-safety experts emphasize the need to supervise young children when space heaters are in use. You will have to take into consideration the type of heater—especially whether or not it shuts off automatically when tipped over—and the age of your child. Is the heater located in a safe place? Since there are certain hazards involved in using *any* space heater, please use this question as a reminder to check out the safety of your own.

WHAT SHOULD YOU DO IF...

YOU ARE ALONE IN A
ROOM WITH A SPACE
HEATER?

_____

_____

_____

_____

The presence of the chair in this drawing is a sign of the additional hazard to a small child of climbing up to reach an appliance. The child could tip over the electric coffeepot in attempting to take care of the smoking toaster.

There are other safety clues in this picture. First, when unplugging an appliance (such as the coffeepot), always unplug it from the wall, not from the appliance. Second, when pulling out a plug, never pull it by the cord but always by the plug itself. Third, never try to pry a piece of toast out of a toaster with a fork or other metal object.

WHAT WOULD YOU DO IF...

THE TOASTER WAS
SMOKING?

_____

_____

_____

_____

In answering this question, a lot depends on the age of your child and the age of your television set. Some very young children can adjust their sets better than I can. The question is whether you want your child to touch the set at all; and if so, which dials do you consider safe to touch and which should be left completely alone.

WHAT WOULD YOU DO IF...

THE TV STARTED BLINKING?

_____

_____

_____

_____

63

WHAT WOULD YOU DO IF...

_____

_____

_____

_____

WHAT WOULD YOU DO IF...

WHAT WOULD YOU DO IF...

_____

_____

_____

_____

66

Strangers

Of all the problems covered in this book, dealing with strangers is perhaps the most difficult. It's relatively easy to explain to children the dangers inherent in playing with fire or crossing a busy street. It's harder to explain why a nice-looking person offering candy or a toy is someone to be avoided. The hardest part of all is to do this effectively, yet without creating a fear of everyone and everything that is unfamiliar.

I think this technique of deciding beforehand on a specific, always-to-be-followed way of responding to a particular situation will help children protect themselves without feeling that they need to be fearful whenever they are on the streets.

In recent years we have learned, often painfully, that not all child molesters are strangers. Nevertheless, it seemed best to cover these "What would you do if . . . ?" questions in this section. Needless to say, different parents will want to discuss this subject with their children in different ways. But that's what this book is all about.

Here's an easy one to start with.

WHAT WOULD YOU DO IF...

YOU SAW A STRANGE DOG OR CAT IN YOUR NEIGHBORHOOD?

_____

_____

_____

_____

69

Most of you have made arrangements for a child who regularly must come home before you or another adult is in the house. This picture would illustrate what you want your child to do in an unexpected situation. I put the question in the section on strangers just to indicate one related hazard.

WHAT WOULD YOU DO IF...

YOU CAME HOME AND
FOUND NO ONE AT
HOME?

_____

_____

_____

It may be easy to say, "Don't open the door to strangers," but a person who says he's delivering the mail or a package—or, most persuasive of all, someone who says he's been sent by a parent who is hurt—may not seem like a "stranger" to a child. Before you decide what the answer to this question should be, be sure to take this possibility into consideration. And please let your children know that, if something ever happened to you, you would *never* send a stranger to get them, but would always get the message to them through an adult they know.

WHAT WOULD YOU DO IF...

SOMEONE RANG THE
DOORBELL AND NOBODY
WAS AROUND TO ANSWER
BUT YOU?

_____

_____

_____

_____

Child-safety experts offer these suggestions to children for dealing with strangers who pull up in a car to ask directions:

- Never get near the car. Stand a good ten feet away, at least.
- Stand *diagonally* in *front* of the car door. If the person opens the door, it will act as a partial barrier between you and the car.
- If the stranger does open the door, run.
- If the stranger talks softly or mumbles, ask him to speak up—but don't go near the car. If he won't speak up, run.

WHAT WOULD YOU DO IF...

A CAR PULLED UP TO
ASK DIRECTIONS?

_____

_____

_____

_____

75

Of course you don't want your children to be so frightened of people that they won't say hello to a friendly stranger. I guess you need to explain the difference between a friendly greeting and an unusual or inappropriate offer.

WHAT WOULD YOU DO IF...

A STRANGER OFFERED YOU
CANDY, MONEY, OR GUM?

_____

_____

_____

_____

Unfortunately, not all child molesters are strangers. This makes keeping safe more complicated. Recently a local boy and his friend were walking home from school, when a man down the street called to them from inside his house. He offered them candy and invited them in. The boys had been properly warned; they ran home and told their parents. The parents called the police, who brought mug shots for the boys to look at. The man had previously been charged with rape.

WHAT WOULD YOU DO IF...
A PERSON YOU'VE SEEN IN
YOUR NEIGHBORHOOD ASKED
YOU TO GO WITH THEM TO
SEE SOMETHING SPECIAL?

_____
_____
_____

If it's difficult to deal with the whole issue of child molesting, it's even more difficult to face the fact that not all molesters are strangers. The "Dear Abby" column lately has published many letters from parents confessing that their children have been molested by family members and friends, virtually under the parents' nose. Abby advises that your children should tell you if *anybody* touches them in a place that makes them feel uncomfortable.

WHAT WOULD YOU DO IF...

SOMEONE TOUCHED YOU
IN A PLACE THAT MADE
YOU FEEL UNCOMFORTABLE?

_____

_____

_____

_____

81

WHAT WOULD YOU DO IF...

_____

_____

_____

_____

WHAT WOULD YOU DO IF...

83

Dear Reader,

Do you have any What Would You Do If...? safety questions that you would like to share with other parents? If so, please send them to me at this address:

Mrs. Jeanne Ebert
℅ Houghton Mifflin Company
2 Park Street
Boston, MA 02108

Thank you!